To

From

simple truths for

TEENS

new seasons™
a division of Publications International, Ltd.

Original inspirations by:
Marie Jones, Jennifer John Oullette, June Stevenson.

Photo credits:
Front cover: **Telegraph Colour Library/FPG International**.
FPG International: Laurance B. Aiuppy; Frank Cezus; Jeff Divine; James Mara;
Chris Mooney; Diane Padys; Miguel S. Salmeron; Stephen Simpson;
Telegraph Colour Library; Carl Vanderschuit; VCG; **SuperStock**.

Manufactured in China.

8 7 6 5 4 3 2 1

0-7853-4899-9

HAVE THE COURAGE to use your hopes and imagination as you turn away from the security of childhood and face the unknown realm of adulthood.

Part of the fun of being a teenager
is getting to take part in so many "firsts"—first date,
first car, first job, first vote. It is a time of new experiences
to be savored and enjoyed.

simple truths: teen

WHEN PLANNING YOUR career, listen to your heart and your mind: One will tell you what you really want to do and the other will help you know what is possible. Thereby you will find happiness and success.

BECOMING A TEEN is like hang gliding.
With a few running steps, the days of childhood
are left behind on the ground and
the future is limitless sky.

THE TEENAGE YEARS are a time to spread the wings of individuality and fly off toward a horizon of possibility.

BEING A TEEN means standing for something
you believe in, even if your friends don't agree.
Being a teen means being yourself,
even if that makes you different.

TRUE FRIENDS LIKE you for who you are,
not for how you act or what you wear. Cherish these friends.
If you are fortunate, you will grow old together.

simple truths: teen

THE TEENAGE YEARS last about as long as two terms
in office for a U.S. president. So don't rush.
You have plenty of time to do
all the important things.

TEENAGE YEARS CAN be confusing and sometimes even painful.
To handle the rough spots, equip yourself with this idea:
Each experience is stretching and challenging you to be
your best and grow into more than you were before.

Between school, friends, and family obligations, take some quiet time each day to be alone and listen to your inner voice.

IT'S OKAY NOT to know who I am yet
Or to know what my life's all about.
It's all right not to know what my future holds,
I've got plenty of time to find out.

KEEP A POSITIVE attitude about everything you
have to do in life, because sometimes the things
you are most reluctant to try can give you
the greatest satisfaction.

WHEN YOU'RE A teenager, every life event—
good and bad—becomes an opportunity
to grow into who you are.

TREAT LEARNING AS a voyage of discovery and
you will find yourself the captain
of your life's adventure.

BE PROUD OF your organizational skills—the stuff
of legends! The average teenager adroitly juggles school,
study, work, and social and family responsibilities—
more obligations than the average adult.

simple truths: teen

simple truths: teen

SOMETIMES YOUR MOODS will be like a
roller coaster. Go with the ups and downs,
and try to enjoy the ride.

BREAKUPS: THEY SEEM like the end of the world,
yet they help you to be a stronger individual by defining
who you are and pointing you in the direction
of who you will become.

THE IDEA THAT you can't look for love is true.
Don't look for someone to complete you—complete yourself
and the rest will fall into place.

Lɪғᴇ ɪs ғᴜʟʟ of ultra highs and mega-lows
when you are a teenager. Learn how to surf these waves.
You will catch the thrill of coming up on top
at least some of the time.

WHEN YOU PRETEND to be someone you're not,
you are not only robbing yourself but also robbing the world—
for you are a special being, with your own unique gifts
and value for the world.

As HARD AS you may try to fit in, the times when you most comfortably "fit" are when you are yourself.

Don't worry if you feel like you're taking
one step forward and two steps back. Life is a dance.
Teenage years are the time to practice your steps.

WHEN PEOPLE REMARK that you eat as if
your legs are hollow, tell them you are building
a strong foundation for the future.

simple truths: teen

TEENS ARE LIKE tightrope walkers,
balancing the need to be part of a group with
the desire to remain true to themselves.

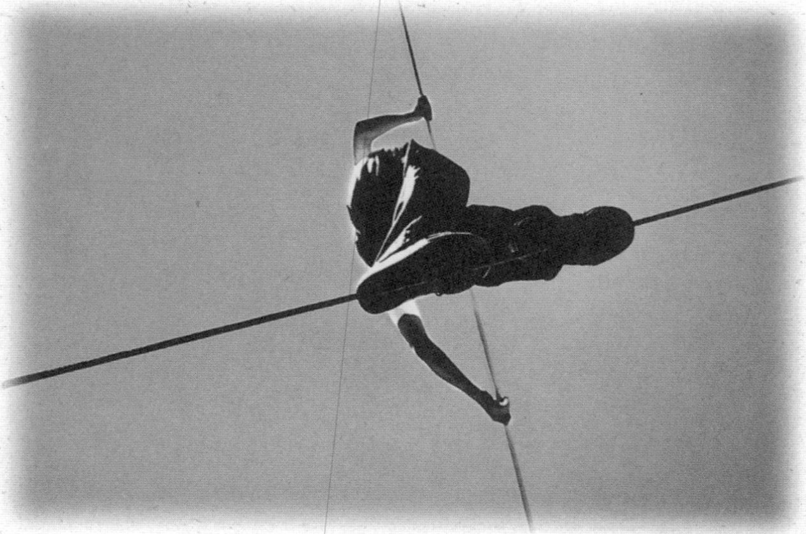

I CAN COUNT on my good friends
When things get rough;
They'll never let me down.
I can turn to my family
When the going gets tough;
They'll always be around.

To SAY YOU have arrived acknowledges the
achievements you have reached at this point in time.
To acknowledge you are on a lifelong journey is
to recognize where you may someday be.

IN LIFE, ALWAYS aim a little farther than you can throw. You might be pleasantly surprised.

THE TEENAGE YEARS are one of the best spans in life.
You are on the bridge between wanting the best and having the best.
Enjoy planning your next move.

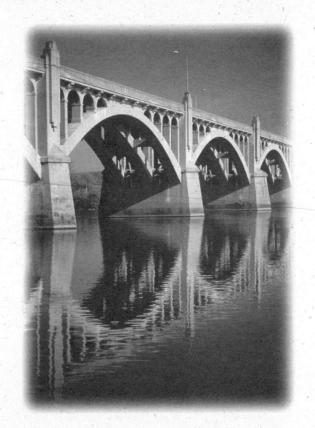

simple truths: teen

WHEN OLDER PEOPLE laugh at the dreams of youth,
remember that they may be regretting the
opportunities they never acted upon.

I<small>T IS NOT</small> the challenges we face
that make us stronger; it is
how we handle them.

LIFE IS LIKE a chess game—
how you play matters
as much as whether
you win or lose.

A TEEN IS like a caterpillar wrapped in the shelter of a cocoon, waiting to break free and become a glorious butterfly.

THE BEST THING about being a teen is knowing that adulthood is a blank slate on which you can draw the life of your imaginings.

Teen Creed

When the winds of life blow,
I'll hang onto myself.
When the road forks in two,
I'll be true to myself.
When the going gets rough,
I'll have faith in myself.
When the journey gets long,
I'll believe in myself.

simple truths: teen

DREAMS CAN BE achieved
when you truly believe—
in your heart.